I Can Measure
Weight at
Any Rate!

Tracy Kompelien

Consulting Editors, Diane Craig, M.A./Reading Specialist
and Susan Kosel, M.A. Education

Published by ABDO Publishing Company, 4940 Viking Drive, Edina, Minnesota 55435.

Printed in the United States.

Credits
Edited by: Pam Price
Curriculum Coordinator: Nancy Tuminelly
Cover and Interior Design and Production: Mighty Media
Photo Credits: Comstock, ShutterStock, Wewerka Photography

Library of Congress Cataloging-in-Publication Data

Kompelien, Tracy, 1975-
    I can measure weight at any rate / Tracy Kompelien.
      p. cm. -- (Math made fun)
    ISBN 10 1-59928-519-3 (hardcover)
    ISBN 10 1-59928-520-7 (paperback)

    ISBN 13 978-1-59928-519-1 (hardcover)
    ISBN 13 978-1-59928-520-7 (paperback)
    1. Mensuration--Juvenile literature. I. Title. II. Series.

QA465.K655 2007
530.8--dc22

                                                          2006017371

SandCastle Level: Transitional

SandCastle™ books are created by a professional team of educators, reading specialists, and content developers around five essential components—phonemic awareness, phonics, vocabulary, text comprehension, and fluency—to assist young readers as they develop reading skills and strategies and increase their general knowledge. All books are written, reviewed, and leveled for guided reading, early reading intervention, and Accelerated Reader® programs for use in shared, guided, and independent reading and writing activities to support a balanced approach to literacy instruction. The SandCastle™ series has four levels that correspond to early literacy development. The levels help teachers and parents select appropriate books for young readers.

Emerging Readers
(no flags)

Beginning Readers
(1 flag)

Transitional Readers
(2 flags)

Fluent Readers
(3 flags)

These levels are meant only as a guide. All levels are subject to change.

Weight is

the measure of how heavy something is.

Words used to describe weight:
**heavier
lighter
ounce
pound
scale**

The  is heavier than the .

If something is heavier, it weighs more.

The  is lighter than the ⬤ .

If something is lighter, it weighs less.

The left **weighs** the same as the right .

This and this

have the same weight.

A slice of  weighs

about 1 ounce.

An ounce is a unit
of measurement.

A loaf of  weighs about 1 pound.

1 pound is equal to 16 ounces.

I Can Measure Weight at Any Rate!

Kate decided to measure the weight of everything she ate. She started by measuring the weight of her empty plate.

Kate put an apple
on the plate.
She looked at the scale
to check the weight.

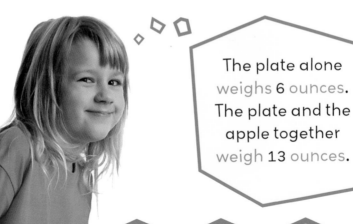

The plate alone
weighs 6 ounces.
The plate and the
apple together
weigh 13 ounces.

Kate ate the apple
and set down the core.
Now the apple is lighter
than it was before!

The plate and the
apple core together
weigh 8 ounces.
So, I ate 5 ounces
of apple!

Measuring Weight Every Day!

My pencil weighs about the same amount as my pen.

Pencils and pens are usually measured in ounces.

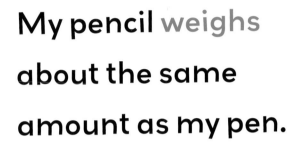

eighteen
18

My eraser weighs less than my notebook.

I measure the weight of my eraser and notebook in ounces.

My desk weighs more than my chair.

I measure the weight of heavier objects in pounds.

twenty-two

22

Would you use pounds or ounces to describe the weight of this small dog?

Glossary

core – the center part of a fruit that you do not eat. Apples and pears are two fruits that have cores.

measure – to determine the size, weight, or capacity of something.

ounce – a unit of measurement in the U.S. customary system.

pound – a unit of measurement in the U.S. customary system. There are 16 ounces in 1 pound.

scale – a tool used to measure weight.